Published by Creative Education and
Creative Paperbacks
P.O. Box 227, Mankato, Minnesota 56002
Creative Education and Creative Paperbacks
are imprints of The Creative Company
www.thecreativecompany.us

Design by The Design Lab
Production by Chelsey Luther
Printed in the United States of America

Photographs by Corbis (Diane McAllister/Nature
Picture Library, Frans Lanting, Yva Momatiuk & John
Eastcott/Minden Pictures, Steven G. Smith, J & C
Sohns/imagebroker), Dreamstime (David Burkes,
Maria Itina), iStockphoto (Gary Alvis, cassp),
National Geographic Creative (MELISSA FARLOW),
Shutterstock (Cattallina, Katrina Leigh, Galushko
Sergey), SuperStock (Biosphoto)

Library of Congress Cataloging-in-Publication Data
Riggs, Kate.
Wild horses / Kate Riggs.
p. cm. — (Amazing animals)
Summary: A basic exploration of the appearance,
behavior, and habitat of wild horses, animals that
roam in bands. Also included is a story from folklore
explaining how people began riding horses.
Includes index.
ISBN 978-1-60818-493-4 (hardcover)
ISBN 978-1-62832-093-0 (pbk)
1. Wild horses—Juvenile literature. 2. Przewalski's
horse—Juvenile literature. 3. Horses—Juvenile literature. I. Title. II. Series: Amazing animals.
SF360.R54 2015
599.665'5—dc23   2013051255

CCSS: RI.1.1, 2, 4, 5, 6, 7; RI.2.2, 5, 6, 7, 10;
RI.3.1, 5, 7, 8; RF.1.1, 3, 4; RF.2.3, 4

First Edition
9 8 7 6 5 4 3 2 1

WILD HORSES

BY KATE RIGGS

CREATIVE EDUCATION · CREATIVE PAPERBACKS

Three kinds of wild horses

live in the world today. Mustangs and brumbies are called wild horses. But they come from horses that people trained long ago. Przewalski's (*sheh-VAWL-skees*) horses have always been wild.

Mustangs are found mainly in the American West

Horses have long necks and large heads. They have a toe called a hoof on each leg. Wild horses have thick hooves. The hooves grow all the time, like human fingernails. But they get worn down on rocks.

A horse may use its head to help relieve itchy skin

Male mustangs are the largest wild horses. They can be 5 feet (1.5 m) tall and weigh 1,000 pounds (454 kg). Most wild horses weigh 500 to 800 pounds (227–363 kg).

When a horse stands on its back legs, it is called rearing

Horses' bodies are covered with hair. A mane runs down the back of a horse's neck. Mustangs have a patch of hair called a forelock. The forelock grows between the ears.

The manes of wild horses are shorter than tame horses'

A group of horses will gather at a watering hole to drink

Horse
teeth are good at cutting grass. Wild horses eat a lot of grass. They eat plant parts like **twigs** and berries, too. Wild horses drink fresh water every day. They drink from running rivers or streams. They drink from still ponds or lakes.

twigs small branches or stems growing from a tree or bush

A foal can stand within one or two hours of its birth

A mother horse usually has one **foal** at a time. Foals are born with their eyes open. They drink milk from their mothers. Foals drink milk for the first few months of their lives. They start eating grass by two weeks of age.

foal a baby horse

A group of horses larger than a band is called a herd

Young horses stay with their mothers and other horses in a **band**. A male horse called a stallion leads the band. Horses can live in the wild for 30 years or more. Przewalski's horses look out for **predators** like wolves.

band a family group of horses

predators animals that kill and eat other animals

*Foals work off their
extra energy by playing*

Wild horses travel around their home range. They eat grass and drink water. Foals chase each other and play. All the horses run away from predators.

home range an area where animals live that has enough food for them to eat

People in western North America can see mustangs. Some people go to Australia to visit brumbies. Przewalski's horses live in protected parts of Mongolia. It is exciting to see wild horses run free!

The United States government works to protect mustangs

A *Wild Horse Story*

How did people first ride wild horses? American Indians used to tell a story about this. Once there was a boy who wanted to help his people hunt. He looked far and wide for animals faster than dogs. Finally, he found the wild horses. He caught the leader and jumped on his back. And the Blackfoot Indians became the best horse riders in the West.

Read More

Heinz, Brian. *Cheyenne Medicine Hat*. Mankato, Minn.: Creative Editions, 2006.

Stanley, George Edward. *Wild Horses*. New York: Random House, 2001.

Websites

San Diego Zoo Animals: Przewalski's Horse
http://animals.sandiegozoo.org/animals/przewalskis-horse
Watch a video of Przewalski's horses at the San Diego Zoo.

Wild Horse Coloring Pages
http://www.hellokids.com/c_21568/coloring-pages/animal-coloring-pages/horse-coloring-pages/wild-horse
Print off pictures of wild horses to color.

Note: Every effort has been made to ensure that the websites listed above are suitable for children, that they have educational value, and that they contain no inappropriate material. However, because of the nature of the Internet, it is impossible to guarantee that these sites will remain active indefinitely or that their contents will not be altered.

Index